D1123324

Nature's Cycles
Animals

Dana Meachen Rau

Marshall Cavendish
Benchmark
New York

A dog was once a puppy. A cat was once a kitten. Baby animals grow up to be adult animals. Adult animals have more babies. That is called a *life cycle*.

Some babies come out of a mother's body. These animals are *mammals*.

Baby chipmunks are pink and tiny when they are first born. Soon, they will grow fur and open their eyes.

Some babies start from eggs.
Eggs can be hard. A baby
lizard has to crack open an
egg to get out.

Some eggs are soft. Fish lay soft eggs in the water.

Tiny fish, called *fry*, come out and start to swim.

Babies need food! A mother bird brings worms to her *hatchlings*. A little caterpillar munches on leaves. A young fox drinks its mother's milk.

Some babies look a lot like their parents. They are just smaller. A foal looks like a horse.

A baby monkey looks a lot like his mother.

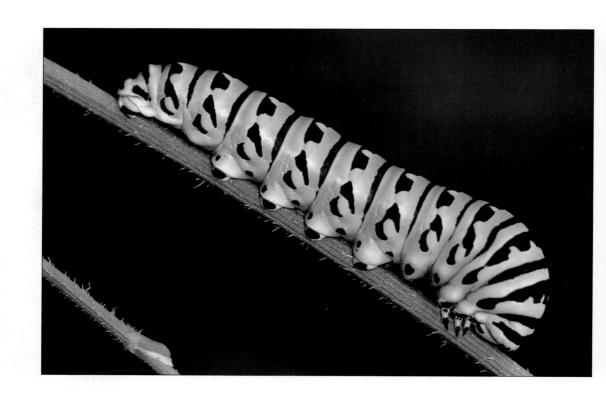

Other babies do not look like their mothers at all! A caterpillar is a baby butterfly or moth.

A tadpole is a baby frog.

Some babies do not need their mothers. *Newborn* snakes and lizards go out to live on their own.

Other babies stay with their mothers. A kangaroo carries her baby in a pouch.

The mother teaches her baby how to live. A lioness teaches her cubs how to hunt.

A mother crane shows her chicks how to fly. Babies stay with their mothers until they can live on their own.

Food helps all animals grow. Growing means changing. Young animals will grow to become adults. Boy animals are called *males*. Girl animals are called *females*.

A male and female greet each other. They might do a dance. They might show off. Then they *mate*. Mating is making more babies.

Some babies grow inside
the female. A hamster grows
inside its mother for more than
two weeks.

An elephant grows inside its mother for almost two years. When the baby is big enough, the female gives *birth*.

Some females lay eggs. Babies grow inside the eggs outside of the female's body.

The babies *hatch* out of the eggs.

Some animals give birth to one baby at a time. Other anmals have many. A dolphin has one baby.
A spider lays 100 eggs!
The life cycle starts again.

Challenge Words

birth (burth)—When a live baby comes out of a mother's body.

females (FEE-males)—Girl animals.

fry—Baby fish.

hatch—To break out of an egg.

hatchlings—Baby birds or other animals that come out of an egg.

life cycle (life SY-kuhl)—The series of things that happen over and over again as a baby is born, grows, and has more babies.

males—Boy animals.

mammals—Animals that have hair or fur, give birth to live young, and drink mother's milk.

mate—To make babies.

newborn—Just born from an egg or a mother's body.

Index

Page numbers in **boldface** are illustrations.

*The author would like to thank Paula Meachen
for her scientific guidance and expertise in reviewing this book.*

With thanks to Nanci Vargus, Ed.D., and Beth Walker Gambro, reading consultants

Marshall Cavendish Benchmark
99 White Plains Road
Tarrytown, New York 10591-9001
www.marshallcavendish.us

Library of Congress Cataloging-in-Publication Data

Rau, Dana Meachen, 1971–
Animals / by Dana Meachen Rau.
p. cm. — (Bookworms. Nature's cycles)
Includes index.
Summary: "Introduces the idea that many things in the world around us are cyclical in nature and discusses the life cycle of animals—how they grow, mate, and procreate"—Provided by publisher.
ISBN 978-0-7614-4093-2
1. Animal life cycles—Juvenile literature. I. Title.
QL49.R358 2009
590—dc22
2008042513

Editor: Christina Gardeski
Publisher: Michelle Bisson
Designer: Virginia Pope
Art Director: Anahid Hamparian

Photo Research by Anne Burns Images

Cover Photo by *Peter Arnold, Inc.*/Klein

The photographs in this book are used with permission and through the courtesy of:
Peter Arnold, Inc.: pp. 1, 15 Ed Reschke; p. 2 WILDLIFE; p. 8 Klaus Jost; p. 17 Roland Seitre; p. 18 BIOS Michel & Christine Denis-Huot; p. 23 BIOS/Matt Alexander; p. 28 Jonathan Bird. *Photo Researchers*: p. 5 Tom McHugh; p. 13 Dr. P. Marazzi; pp. 26, 27 E. R. Degginger. *Animals Animals*: p. 6 Zigmund Leszczynski; p. 9 David Dennis; p. 19 Tom Lazar; p. 24 Fabio Medeiros Colombini; p. 25 Klaus-Peter Wolf. *Corbis*: p. 11 Lightscapes Photography, Inc.; p. 16 David A. Northcott. *Getty Images*: p. 12 John Kelly; p. 14 altrendo nature; p. 20 Freudenthal Verhagen.

Printed in Malaysia
1 3 5 6 4 2

10/12   E
590
RAU